GRANITE
DIVES

The New Issues Press Poetry Series

Editor	Herbert Scott
Associate Editor	David Dodd Lee
Advisory Editors	Nancy Eimers, Mark Halliday
	William Olsen, J. Allyn Rosser
Assistant to the Editor	Rebecca Beech
Assistant Editors	Allegra Blake, Matthew Hollrah,
	Alexander Long, Amy McInnis,
	Tony Spicer, Tom West
Editorial Assistants	Laura Maloney, Lydia Melvin, Bonnie Wozniak
Business Manager	Michele McLaughlin
Fiscal Officer	Marilyn Rowe

The New Issues Press Poetry Series is sponsored by The College
of Arts and Sciences, Western Michigan University, Kalamazoo, Michigan

First Edition, 1999.

ISBN: 0-932826-88-1 (paperbound)

Library of Congress Cataloging-in-Publication Data:
Rabb, Margaret
Granite Dives/Margaret Rabb
Library of Congress Catalog Card Number (99-076767)

Art Direction:	Tricia Hennessy
Design:	Sarah Folck
Production:	Paul Sizer
	The Design Center, Department of Art
	College of Fine Arts
	Western Michigan University
Printing:	Courier Corporation

GRANITE
DIVES

MARGARET RABB

New Issues Press

WESTERN MICHIGAN UNIVERSITY

For my daughters, lights of my eyes.

Dust as we are, the immortal spirit grows
Like a harmony in music; there is a dark
Inscrutable workmanship that reconciles
Discordant elements . . .

                             . . . Back I cast a look,
And lingered near the door a little space,
Then sought with quiet heart my distant home.

                —William Wordsworth
                The Prelude

Contents

Open Air

Air Failure

Underwater Lights

The Struggle Back

Acknowledgments

Many thanks to the editors of the publications where these poems first appeared:

Alligator Juniper: "Dame Julian in a Hazelnut"

Carolina Quarterly: "At Chartres," "Mustard Greens"

Christianity and Literature: "Night Drive"

Columbia: A Journal of Literature and Art: "The Long and Short of It"

The Comstock Review: "Phantom Pantoum"

Flyway: "Penelope:"

Georgetown Review: "A Seasoning in Hell," "Clover Anaphora," "Vermeer Interiors"

The Greensboro Review: "Self-Portrait with Paintbrush"

The Kenyon Review: "To Autumn"

Literal Latté: "Family Receipts"

Louisiana Literature: "Retired Couples View Pompeii," "Reverie in Silk Hope, North Carolina," "Dogwood Alarm"

Lullwater Review: "On Melancholy Again"

The Madison Review: "At the Mothers of Twins Club, 1984," "Honeysuckle," "Parent," "Cruel Lament for Elms"

Poetry Daily: "Cape Lookout" (www.poems.com)

Solo: "Uffizi Repetitions," "What Are You Saying"

Sow's Ear Poetry Review: "Low Owl Illusion"

sub-TERRAIN: "Quitting Byzantium"

The Wildwood Journal: "Five Short Songs to Eurydice"

A group of these poems was also published in *Figments of the Firmament*, the 1998 North Carolina Writers' Network Harperprints Chapbook selection judged by Richard Jackson, and two appeared in *The Denny Poems* volumes for 1995-1996 and 1997-1998. "Dogwood Alarm" was included in *Word and Witness, 100 Years of North Carolina Poetry*, edited by Sally Buckner. "Night Drive" was selected for Salem College's Poems in Public Places.

Several poems were recognized on first publication, winning the *Louisiana Literature* Prize for Poetry, the Phyllis Smart Young Award, the Hackney Literary Award, the *Sow's Ear* poetry contest, the *Columbia* winter poetry competition, the *Lullwater* Prize for Poetry, the Last Poems Prize, the Guy Owen/Tom Walters poetry contest at NC State University, the Tunstall Prize from the Chrysler Museum of Art, a *Literal Latté* poetry award, a Wildwood Prize, and a Galway Kinnell Award.

Work on the poems in this volume was made possible by fellowships and residencies from The Headlands Center for the Arts, Writers Conferences and Festivals (AWP), the North Carolina Arts Council, The North Carolina Writers' Network, the Sewannee Writers' Conference and the Wesleyan Writers Conference. Profound thanks for these and for all the generosity which has sustained this writing.

Open Air

Low Owl Illusion

Early but already broad daylight this morning
a barred owl glided across the path, so close I saw
wing edges split by a broken shaft, a feathery flaw,
and thin claws that trailed like exposed wiring.
Halfway up a poplar she lit by a nubbly opening,
slipped inside a gap healed around a lost limb's raw
socket, and sank instantly into the dark hollow,
all but her tail, like a bracket on the bark, a warning.
At the high end of hearing, voices thin as a wafer
bled from the tree. She squeezed back out, turned
on me her great fixed eyes and stared down: *You.*
She held still, but the longer I looked, the less I saw her.
I mean, it was only by blinking back the form I yearned
for that she stayed in view at all, whatever she was and who.

Honeysuckle

A shock: the shift from one
breath to the next.
Because she was running
it hit her open mouth:
an airy bath, a tubfull dashed
down her throat. It choked
her back to last May and the last,
to someone she might marry.
They ambled past children, past
houses, through a weedy
garden. They talked across the path,
a paraphrase of energy
as delight, a force or field
sweetened to shake out shape.
With one step the flood
poured over, white bell
flower foam, ions
charging from hollows.
In three feet they left
its channel—a wonder
any sense persists
the same—drowned, caught back,
deluged, awake again.

Reverie in Silk Hope, North Carolina

In Ottoman Turkey, village women slipped
Spinning silkworms down their bodices
And buttoned up when the temperature dropped.

Incubated close in the radiant interstices
Of garments, the delicate pupae wove on.
Cocooned, pillowed, plush, they jetted

A thin thread, harsh yellow, in bovine
Concentration. Thus, a woman vetted
By her father for a future husband gazes

Past the Anatolian plain. Her index fingers
Remember how to unwind the sticky cases
She grows, attached to a rib that hungers

For a high, flat pattern, a rug geometry
Of layers: bordered, stepped, reduced
From the sacks that swell on her body.

The constellations would appear confused
If she woke in the cool of our night
To find the stars turned, or herself spun

Under humid piedmont air. She'd catch a tiny
Rustle of wings stretched over the ganglion
That carpets her heart. The touch means a moth

Like a nova, a bright speck in the distance,
Is about to leave the larva in its winding cloth
For the stone-splashed plateau of happenstance.

The Tidal Bore

It was a kid's summer vacation thing to do
like getting up at six for the Reversing Falls'
whirls and eddies—take a chance on boredom
or eccentric amusement and drive upriver
from St. Johns where we wait for the fun
behind the brick ranch Cy's Seafood Rest-

> aurant on a patch of damp grass, a rest
> over the rippled riverbed now subdued to
> a trickle that runs down to the Bay of Fundy
> with its four-story tides. A mud flat stench falls
> around the banks where tube worms live
> in duckweed and clumps of false hellebore.

Other watchers drift in. We see Bore
Park upstream packed, more interest
than we dreamed possible in a fluke river.
Our cohorts with coolers make a to-do
over how much the water table falls
every year so the old four-foot abundance

> that ripped along fifty miles from Fundy
> when they were children, the true tidal bore,
> is dwindled to a foot. Now the current falls
> off, dammed above Moncton, pressed
> into a lake for a ring of big frou-frou
> houses built for people down on a river.

Heraclitus himself dipped a toe in no river
twice, cut no slack for the tide of funda-
mentalists, had their cake and ate it, too, do
you see, one foot washed up where he bore
his logo canoe on portage from flux to rest
in a flame of wit lit under the waterfalls.

We forget why we're here; my daughter falls
asleep, squinting against the glare off the river
where nothing changes, or all, a point of rest—
when we hear a gull, smell the salt from Fundy,
and the ocean, ancient and diminished, that bore
us onto land, rushes inland, a wall of water to do

whatever there is to do when a creature falls
past boredom, wakes, rights a canoe in the river
and, new found, seeks a broken surf to bear the rest.

Rock Reader

Brick layer, stone mason, rock man in the north Georgia buckeye hill towns

an hour up from Atlanta, the old uncle crushed and ground his vowels

to a fine silt until he hardly need open his mouth to speak, invoked sounds

sustained by a drone down his throat, uttered from eyes, nose, lips, brows,

volcanic, sclerotic, a lava and rubble river, baseline fault chant, tone that drowns

sense sieved through the cells, burlap vocal cord of tomtom, shells and growls.

Water that courses over the rapids, he croons, runs pure as it spins past the ninth stone

or when it rides the three gold horses, the same who drank here in blood, flesh and bone.

Famous for some miles, he renders buried signs with a divining wire held in place,

cuts a green branch to carry the charge, pull, jerk, and stop cold over mud or sand

where he digs with nails and sticks, afraid to risk a shovel blade on the hidden face.

First he finds the eye, it draws his gaze, flaked from the stone, broken out by hand,

then sees around it a lizard shape, a bear's head, a swollen profile of the older race

that stands in a cave below or dark spring nearby, a map to show the lay of the land

the way it was fixed a thousand years ago when all the animals slipped away

and quit this thicket of bird points and secret chips, dirt dishes from red clay.

Acre-long mounds break the leaf cover to expose an
undulation, pattern perfect

in detail as one drawn on a bowl glazed in ground copper
with a fine pointed brush

of the painter's hair bound on a stem, serpentine, verdant
skinned, scaled to deflect

age like a gulleywasher watershed worn smooth, a magnified
memory of rattle-rush

when pulse pumps back and pupils dilate. If God is the eye
of heaven, this wrecked

artifact, millennia overgrown, survives for God alone, the
vision of our coldest wish.

Let those who dug in the river basins and hauled earth to the
ramparts repose unknown,

held as their souls behold the hot sky from this knot garden
bulwark, snake seed resown.

Ask him and the old rock reader will tell you the way to hunt
arrowheads down:

walk a field just turned, before the harrow breaks the clods;
come back the way you went

in the same furrow; aim for late afternoon in November,
when the sun hits the ground

straight along the horizon line; scan your own height ahead
since no one can spot flint

or obsidian at their feet. It all hangs on the angle of light to
eye, the broken land around,

your slantwise glance. Stay so long you forget whatever there
was to find, when the glint

off a razor edge drags you down the row. Pick up a chalk white
speck, damp in the solid day.

It waits over dark tillage, sessile, subsiding, found to any hand it
fits, settled in sound you say.

The Long and Short of It

Enclosed, I'm sending my last snap of Joe
it was years ago
your brother looked so much like you, red
and freckled, light headed
tickled to death behind a camera to shoot for you
an antic, pregnant view
of my body stretched, enormous with child.
He laughed like wild
when I balanced a dinner plate on the bulge
so he could divulge
and amuse: how odd I appeared in profile, caught
prenatal and overwrought
like a polychrome madonna who expected less of her lover
(when is this over?)
than she got. That was the year Joe moved to Atlanta
and became the *infanta*
terrible of the gay scene there, stylish and mannered
so I heard
and saw for myself over his airy charm, a hilarity
studied in the city.
But you were already out of the Smokies in LA
not in Cherokee, anyway.
Back east, the ultrasound outlined two blips of bodies
twins on a fluid breeze
the way a scan his last year zeroed three spots on his brain
proof of more pain.
What Joe found out while I raised two children
was how to love all men
to adore with his body as Christ with his heart
spoke every part
to suffer and be buried, descend and be the next day
riven, born clean away.

Family Receipts

Honey, I want to fix us a long, narrative
supper, six courses, each with a new sauce,
a mind its own you unfurl north to south
on the white tablecloth like a sheet of paper
set with beautiful silver characters free
of deep meaning, just folds and water rings

where the glasses bead, waiting for the rings
to come off, to plunge hands in a narrative
of butter kneaded into flour until it's free
floating like seeds in snow powder, sauce
apples hard and black skinned, sliced paper
thin so you can read news of home, the south,

clean through them: nuclear storage in South
Carolina, tainted groundwater seeping in rings
from Barnwell. The price is high; the newspaper
allows how they put it all into schools, a narrative
tone to calm and detox, drench us in white sauce,
a prose hollandaise. We know nothing's free

of course; as children we read about others' free
form years with mixed pickle rancor and old south
distance, dragged out our vowels longer, sauce
hotter. Now nothing on the network news rings
true or tastes right. Even God's truth is narrative;
it needs to wander loose before you grind new pepper

into salty flour, shake the chicken legs in a paper
bag and slide them in a spitting skillet. Drained free
on newsprint, they pick up a tinge of type, a narrative
in backward letters, smudged, lead like the sorry south
in the mouth of a reporter, out after gravy, running rings
around us. Well. For dessert we'll spoon raspberry sauce

over pound cake with boiled custard, a sauced sauce,
and light candles to keep off the mosquitoes. Paper
winged moths will circle treasure in corrupted rings,
our rusted table, till we steal inside to break them free
and brew a pot of strong coffee. We're not in the south
here, we just brought along okra seeds and a narrative

sense of narrative order, the story of dish and sauce
from great aunts, south sayers, recipes their only paper,
meringues their heaven, a free, sweet rise to the throne's first rings.

Over the St. Croix River, 1957

After the Red Owl grocery and ten squares of Hershey bar
Jane's mother stopped the car at the Indian mounds
above the river on the Wisconsin side, a park and grounds
with benches, kept at public expense but not popular.
The pavement gave way to cracked macadam tar;
ankle-high cinquefoil and bent grass crept around
concrete posts swagged with chain that she wound,
swung and hung upside down from, to start a circular
skin-the-cat over to the other side. She ran, she fled
toward the round hills, a long row of knees raised
from the bluff, and dashed up the first steep grade.
The top, nearly flat, opened like an apron, spread
a lap where she lay back. Blue ebbed to gray as she stared
then rolled longways down, arms overhead, sun struck and flared.

Jane spun too fast to feel the straw grass jab her side
till it wrapped a rough scratchy skin around her,
a flea bitten bear robe turned inside out, coarse fur
rubbed in some acorn oil to stain and tan her hide.
She gets to her feet and sprints up the next slope—
maybe twenty strides but her breath pulls and knocks.
How can she stop herself now from the first dream step
onto the current that raises birds over the river, that rocks
her over bluff and gravel in air like silt of a deep cold well.
The draft rushes under her arms and streams through hair
grown long and black. A keening rises as four dugouts clear
the bend, logs burned hollow and shaped for this channel.
The canoes turn and arrow into shore, scraping the shallows;
then bright dark figures lift the dead toward their barrows.

Mustard Greens

Before I-40 I pass the Minnis back pasture,
a hill sprung up in mustard where women in a row
pick greens into brown grocery bags the first pure
March days. This morning it flowers a livid vicious yellow
over the tough stems they left and the sons have turned
their black angus out to graze: a rough draft, a puncture:
sloe, midnight, scattered singly on the bright ground
that slants up to a sky blown straight back to blue.

I bear in mind my father, a part in his thin hair, pressed
flat black over papery skin, where combed tines were afraid
to slip. I knew he could punch and core the earth's crust
with us, die-cut holes cow or crow shaped, double bladed,
blank and vacant where we just stood, betraying this minute,
driving the lush surface, how fast it will flip to its opposite.

At the Mothers of Twins Club, 1984

Each belly still a loose net
from the big stretch, we met
at eight in a church basement,
linoleum scuffed dull as we felt.

We sat in damp cloth chairs to talk
about how to settle and hold apart
fretful babies in a grocery cart
and still leave room for milk;

or to lie in bed some easy way
and nurse at midnight two tiny
mouths; then what to say
to the relentless query

("No, one's a spare—they break,")
the pouts and sulks that the names
don't rhyme, ploys to shake
off pinchers, pokers, strangers

who sport and grimace in our faces.
We flitted giddy, slap happy
to hear the others' worst cases,
their whiny, bumper sticker misery—

Twins Are Two Much—turned plumb
witty on the round edge of exhaustion.
Our poached breasts had begun
their telltale pitch: *Go home*

or pop. Out in the parked car
my nether self sways in the dark
passenger seat, that familiar star
of silent address, habitual mark

for my inner narration, sister
in daily minutiae. She nods twice,
leans shoulder to my shoulder
so I feel between us a cell's choice,

see everyone split, one of a pair,
double, identical ova tied
hair for hair to the very very
same on the other, louvered side.

Air Failure

The Gingerbread Orrery

In a dark kitchen the two girls enter,
ideas for a mobile glow and hover
already half-baked, iced blue or bitter
yellow, hung from a rafter
strung on whisper florist wire.
Ingredients spill along the counter:
molasses, milk, soda, salt, flour.
The girls slide the metal beater
into an old white standing mixer,
cream, spin, crack an egg on the batter,
then stir by hand the hard nebular
spiral too thick for any motor;
they add cinnamon, powdered ginger,
nutmeg scraped on a minute grater,
dust clouds poured over one another
on the terra cotta mound. Chill one hour.
They wash bowls, run warm water
over dabs of dough that linger,
then cut a cardboard pattern cipher
for each planet, ring and lunar.
The sun, counterweight to all, a danger
so huge, flared and hot beyond measure,
it could char us to cinders in one flicker,
they splice with a second layer
of clear tape and heavy paper.
They take the cooled spicy sphere
from the icebox, its own winter,
roll it to a thin brown platter,
trim celestial bodies for the fire
and set them baking in a figure
of the rising big bang matter.
A smooth surface cracks a fissure
and dents into a thumbprint crater

spread on the cooling rack of nature.
The girls whip egg whites into sugar
and tint the frosting to match each color
in their book: red for Mars, Jupiter ocher,
Venus turquoise, Neptune blue, Pluto darker.
The sun by now a marbled orange fever
too heavy to hang by a thread in air
they cradle in a star of wire.
Then from a dowel sprayed with glitter
they string nine globes in sober order
stretched out from the cornered solar.
Let no wind rock the perfect scatter
of that mother, by that father.

A Seasoning in Hell

Carolina pit barbeque restaurant decor
invariably celebrates les cochons d'enfer.

Bandsawn plywood, cross stitched, sheet metal
porkers hang as worldly signs of a satiate cabal.

These aren't just happy pigs, either, apple
smugly stuffed, self satisfied on the platter.

Rather, these ecstatic swine lift meek forelegs
to praise Jesus who made divine mere shreds

And sauce. Amen, hogs. Dance on, shoulder
to shoulder, cheek by jowl, let hocks shudder,

Let hickory flames rise around you, consume
all flesh until it sputters into burnt communion.

Pass through living coals, brothers, leap after
each other, doused in vinegar and cayenne pepper.

Run two sheets before the wind, sanctify and seize
the flame azalea, its incense wasted bateau epiphanies.

Your bête noir serves the side dishes with a devilish
grin and spins the tray: red hot hell bent damn dervish.

Resistant to heat

to drought, scale and vermin
red-flagged at their margin
seeds dry their thick carmine
in the cicadas' high engine.

The green furze of nightshade
sharp-staked to the backstay
vents its poison leaf tirade
a martyr's bouquet.

All August my doldrums
pinched back by Plato
ripen in tantrums
one racy tomato.

Night Drive

Just past dark seven deer cross the road.
As the last three turn back from a field
headlights kindle their eyes.
Walkway lamps circle a farmhouse,
about to carry it off. This afternoon
someone mowed the shoulder
so stem and seed sharpen the air.
Step down the brights.
How the night deepens—on the wheel
hands are darker than branches.
To travel this way, admit one voice,
low as a motor, dry as cicadas:
> *Where are you going, out so late*
> *Far from home and the close kept gate.*

Parent

Only mother handled knives.
She took them from a drawer of sharps
where dark air knit their knuckled sides.
Some lay straighter, some cast curves,
she picked the paring knife as hers.

Apple peelings sprang in rings
between her blade and thin thumb skin.
She never knicked a pear or broke
open mobius spiralings
to bare a planet's slanted spin.

The edge went out, the metal cold;
she oiled the stone across her knee
then circled steel against the grit:
flipped it, felt it, bent to see
how friction hones and keens its hold.

Only mother flattened rounds
in razor slices with the wrist.
She caught the knack of knocking back
all the covers, then rewound
their knots and knobs to tighter twists.

When she gets tired, she cuts close
and knaps her nails like flinty stones.
Does she not know the knife will linger,
flay the blue veins from her bones—
a little extra, whetted finger?

Penelope:

When he sailed here from Helen's
war he carried Circe in his cells

a smell indelible as tattoo, grounded,
all the other voices siren drowned.

I wasn't that stupid, my fabric woven
and ripped, seasick with worn love.

Two heroic decades last longer
than ten at home. No wrong

track or lost number tunes his body
to the sharp tooled edge some god

tests for his next move, the destroyer
salvaged on the stone field of Troy.

When that ugly lot of suitors
went soft like too ripe fruit

I saw him from my highest window
shaking sailcloth in the sea wind,

sent a glint from my hair, belayed,
combed in the sun like the stay

sheet. Between clay bowls and charcoal
we passed in a market. In that dark

his gray eyes as cool as silver flickered
under salt ash, buried in the kiln.

They ravel the lantern light, cut a pattern
on the absent ocean that ebbs so it can turn,

reflected on harbor water and slow breakers
that wake on their reluctant travels back.

Vermeer Interiors

To pin him down we hang his women like contraband.
Each is lit by a sun, through glass panes on the left wall,
that plays on the letter, pitcher, pen, pearls in her hand,

and exposes his clear washes over her glazed face, fanned
to a glow in the air around her, an eye blink's folderol.
To pin him down we hang his women like contraband

solid as the Spanish chairs with small lion heads that stand
behind her back and look back at her, a finial in thrall
that plays on the letter, pitcher, pen, pearls. In her hand

the paper quakes against a map of the world. Sand
and water divide them. She leans into her pen to scrawl,
to pin him down. We hang his women. Like contraband,

Moses in the bulrushes estranges seas and charted land,
caught by Pharaoh's daughter in the black checked hall.
That plays on the letter. Pitcher, pen, pearls in her hand,

she weighs their beaded fall. The coat (with ermine band)
shows blue or gold. His eye plies hers, the brush carries all.
To pin him down we hang his women like contraband
that plays on the letter, pitcher, pen: pearls in her hand.

What are you saying,

that the sky below
slips black and blue,

tree roots grip
to choke the pipes,

this open window
casts a shadow,

no one tells lies,
ice water rises

through clear air,
stars just aren't there,

old eggs float,
dog backs up God,

I never knew
one half of you.

Five Short Songs to Eurydice

I

The journey down, already over; the struggle
back, almost awake. She climbs through rock
and slag, a shade with mapping soles, a double
of herself Hades breathed in, breathed out, locked

up again. Shackled—or let loose
in beauty denser than what we perceive—
she's an amber bead, a less diffuse
version of everything we leave.

She slides along a filament burnt tight
at either end, picked up on Orpheus' wire
and fused in Pluto's burly malachite.

The tremor of their longing trips her string.
See her!—without will or fire
in orbit between them as they bow and sing.

II

You orbit between them. They bow and sing.
Though you must follow voice or flute
you drag your heels, snake-bit suspicious thing
made both reward and risk. The absolute

took all but given names. You step, repeat
Eurydice, Eurydice. You're rid
of what? Well shut of capital conceit
down south among the headless, stony dead.

From a bedrock couch by a tangy red oak root
you hear the surf of traffic as it wears
the surface world. At any minute

a long haul diesel will shift and strain to make
the grade. The slow release of downhill gears
rumbles to you over Styx' dammed lake.

III

He stumbled over Styx, its manmade lake
of hatred flocked and dumbstruck at hell's bells.
Should this atone? She weathered in his wake,
was towed behind his truck in grease and smells

of flooded engines, hooked and pulled to dustrags,
wanton laundry, dishes, red wine hang-
overs, mopping up. She heeds his zigzags,
hairpin turns of phrase, sharp words in lang-

uage to die for. Rainer Maria Rilke, will
you turn around? I dare you not to kill
her twice, two-timing the poet's oath. Welt

raised in her throat, she carries grief
that rings your voice, herself a missed and brief
form, a slip won below the earth's black belt.

IV

For his one dip below the earth's black belt
you daily offer up a spectral tune.
Through trees that sway asleep in ears, he felt
the notes of animals bleed into his doom.

We know by now that love's a certain order,
a genus of death, the empty set.
Orpheus will call himself your mourner,
the one who praises on the clarinet.

You send him wind that moves past, over nothing
at all—no tongue, no reed, no lung, no string.
No letter, cathode, page or ray. Erase

to null Hades' dark print shop, manuscripts
thick with secret ink. Wash his lips
to blank new vellum. Incite outer space.

V

On blank blue velvet inside outer space
nothing can remind her of the past.
She holds no purchase there, and finds each face
without relation, new, obviously last.

By contrast, the stylist at the underworld
salon says "You're the third woman today
who said she wants her hair cut and curled
to look less like her mother," gone to gray

and tarnished in the mirror. While she sleeps
moonshine in Hades seeps from pores of rocks,
a closet firmament, a fountain box.

She's cool as aquifers, fluid in the deeps.
In afterlife she's a daughter lost to trouble,
the journey down already over struggle.

Underwater Lights

Damascus Fugue State

Blackberry winter covers the brambles, lying
as if it doesn't belong to the branch. The gravel
underfoot sparks as he steps, shot with pyrite.
He hears a fool's gold voice, his name but lighter
and something like scales falls from his eyes.

Shot with fool's gold, he steps on blackberries.
Under the winter gravel something recovers.
He scales the light here through pyrite sparks,
a voice falls to his eyes. As if it doesn't belong,
a bramble to the branch, a name lies at his feet.

The black spark longs to voice what he hears alight
under a bramble branch. π is a name for the grave,
a cover for his bare gold eyes.
Footsteps fool him to sum all things.
The scale is right for lies to fall, shot in winter.

Light covers black branches as if they are buried
with winter. He falls to his feet, a fool. On the gravel
his steps shoot sparks. He is something right,
but the name doesn't belong to him. He hears a pall
over bramble ice. Gold scales lie in his voice.

Retort from Pétionville

> *And the old casino likewise may define*
> *An infinite incantation of our selves . . .*
> —Wallace Stevens, "Academic Discourse at Havana"

Then this life is an old casino again, cool
behind corrugated metal sheathing past the pool,
lights low, an offset glance on tinted glass and floors,
mermen cut from oil drums floating by the doors.
Haitian croupiers shake their starched white sleeves.
Poison stingers, scales and barbs stick us to the reefs.
With trident rakes they take what change we hold:

Come seven, come eleven, blackjack cashes gold.
Will any good humor man refuse the offer
of rum and raw sugar at his basement altar?
Children gnaw green cane after the embargo.
No aid quenches them, thin-walled and hollow.
Un kou de foudr' catches their red hot pitch, a rout
by the dead who know how best to cast us out.

A lizard drops to my hand, an easy mark
as I unlock my hotel room in the dark,
generators out again. It is the lightest touch,
talk not meant for pages, a slurred language
of slaves, French gone far, far south around
the bend on a cotton bolt the West Indies wound,
a vaudou saint stitched flat and double.

Sequins stretch and pucker, dented and subtle
while in the alley earth is ground to a gutter,
soil caught as silt. The rain runs salt water.
A motor revs and starts to spin. Let the casino
crack a pane and shed the half-light a window
prints on dirt. Once flicked, the roulette wheel
deals clean blood, stale bread, a final meal.

Self-Portrait with Paintbrush

You block out the four-foot board, lower left, till a place
fits, fixes your hand midstroke. The bristles flex dull
through the handle when you press the ferrule surface
with a finger and tip backward in a dim room full
of volatile spirits. You clutch, you baby your old scrap
palette squeezed and mixed with oils. Look at you now—
primer and pigment on a cheap masonite sheet, ego stopgap
for erratic stubble, early receding hairline, a sharp eyebrow
lifted north, ready to split the way your long lip cuts the cheek.
You recognize those agate gravel eyes mean to crush and annul
what they see as it flashes from every angle, wide shot to oblique.
In this lampblack their flares sweep the air out of your skull.
    Any sinner loves a face that loves him, but you
      adore artifice and its open doors into the blue.

Retired Couples Tour Pompeii

For this quick glimpse they braved the streets of Naples,
the wallet snatchers and Italian drivers:

an afternoon of empire, frescoed apples,
the bowers, thrushes over pagan rivers.

They wander through the drizzled ash, a slightly
salted grit, sedate Vesuvian fallout.

It bathes their five poor senses. Worn thin, sight
dims down in dissolution, rooms of flat-out

excess. Murals map huge appetite
for game and wine, while slaves wind gold in women's

dark hair braids. Nothing middling or petite
addresses blood and knucklebones, their omens.

The tour moves on to the necropolis
outside the city walls, a statue garden

it seems at first, the figures quiet, polite
and fully clothed, volcanic status guarded.

What Flora dancing pierces their slow hearts?
This isn't Williamsburg, though true colonial

and ringed with buses. More than any art
the views of retribution draw the lonely

group tourists. Rome has never honored beauty
that ruins all before it. Husband praises

the finish, liquid rock that poured like eau
de vie and ran red hot through blocks and aisles

of town. Wife says, those people made the couches
they must lie down in lava on. Sweet salve.

Their children, we peel off the fire, blow conches
and gambol, voyeurs calling fate ourselves.

On Melancholy Again

No, even at the millennium the torrents go to Lethe, the streams
　　From Freud clotted with leaves, algae, rusted cars, rotten sticks;
Where you set no foot, the current chokes on recurring dreams
　　Or big money bent to lure a cottonmouth for an easy fix.
We still pass by the herb garden, beer bar, video strip mall
　　Where some Greek trick of light or slight of barbarian mind
　　　　Soaks up the gall the toothless gums spit in a cup.
Send them packing—wolf's bane, nightshade, yew, owl, all;
　　No point not rocking the boat, since shades to shade confined
　　　　Though kissed, faded, drowned or twisted, will wake up.

But when you fall into the black fit, cough blood or worse
　　Watch another hack out bits of lung night by night
Until tributary tears crest the bank and break the wall, immerse
　　Your skin, salted with the acid bile that blocks even twilight,
In the glass green Atlantic breakers swelling and curling toward
the beach:
　　Below, far below the tyrean blue we fathom as mere space
　　　　Cumulus clouds, world peonies, roses revised,
Gather to set the scale, a thousand-point perspective so beyond
speech
　　That it's all distance, though we hold close a well known face
　　　　And let it rave as we gaze a long, long way into its eyes.

You live out there on an island somewhere, double lit by sun
　　And dappled refraction from the ocean that slides through
　　the air
Like headlights a wakeful child follows around bedroom walls,
overrun
　　At last as the sweep of tires passes. What is beautiful is despair,
Dolorous in us, even the land as we look back from the waves, shot
　　Through and through as though skin could disappear and we
　　remain

Afloat, pure in and out, invisible as rays to our
children on the shore.
They look up from their castle shrine, buckets of sand, deep-dug
moat,
And believe we're leaving. The grape will shatter on their
tongue again,
Hung in the clouds as we let them go, before, after,
evermore.

Cape Lookout

The shape of god is a minnow, my sister told me
before we knew what to draw for a ghost.
The water of god is shallow. Ankle-high in the sea
bed, warm, we forgot the edge, the drop and deep coast.

Uffizi Repetitions

The Tribuna Room

Rings of mother of pearl set in painted plaster line the dome,
a simple trompe l'oeil, ever lesser shells grown naive as
fingernails
slipped to their moon pink beds. Stars that fell like sprung snails
glow dim all day behind the skin of young Medici girls at home

hung for the last four centuries around the curling walls,
polychrome
and burnished, layered in enamel oil. A sanguine chain prevails,
rings of mother. Pearls set in painted plaster line the dome,
a simple trompe l'oeil ever lesser, shells grown naive as
fingernails

or as Bronzino, the family portrait man, rendered them—hair
parted plumb,
combed back from wide brows, tired eyes drooped at the outer
trails—
a hothouse of related faces. The pleat that cleaves nose to lip
rarely fails

to repeat its pale dip, a thumbprint. The touch to which we
succumb
rings of mother, of pearls set in painted plaster. Line the dome,
a simple trompe l'oeil, ever lesser shells. Grow naive as
fingernails.

La Madonna della Melagrana

In the center of Botticelli's round painting the holy child pulls a
lucid red seed

from the pomegranate his mother holds like a wrinkled globe,
the old earth

battered, cradled in her hand, her long awful fingers curved to
fit its girth.

He looks up, startled again by the gaze of those who go by
glazed with greed.

Mary glances aside, past the angels with books and baskets of
rose and bead

over the edge of the gilded frame. She recalls the death she saw
at his birth

in the center of Botticelli's round painting. The holy child pulls a
lucid red seed

from the pomegranate his mother holds. Like a wrinkled globe,
the old earth

bursts sorrow's fruit. He squeezes a pip, the juice runs down,
the stain he will bleed.

The shower of light over her sad transparent veil and the winged
boys' faded mirth,

even their wavy hair, lifts them away from this grave field, alloys
their airy worth

with gold. Through snowfall at night we rise off rasped breath
and cold ground, freed

in the center of Botticelli's round painting. The holy child pulls a
lucid red seed

from the pomegranate. His mother holds, like a wrinkled globe,
the old earth.

The View over the Arno

Suffused in sun, sheets of glass replace the canvas where what
we say
about what we see streams into the scene like the archangel's word
at the cup of this U-shaped gallery between salon suites, bright
and blurred.
We break into a marble corridor of windows giving on the river
walkway,

Santo Spirito and the Carmine, where Masaccio, Massolino's protégé
put in wet plaster the cries of Adam and Eve, cast, bent, but not
inured,
suffused in sun. Sheets of glass replace the canvas where what we say
about what we see streams into the scene. Like the archangel's word

the gilt letterforms appeared to Mary reading in the garden one
March day.
This cameo articulation of the absolute split the Tuscan landscape.
With that absurd
lily Gabriel vaulted terraces of olive and vine, struck a row of flame
cedar, heard

her gasp to find it torn half in two between her eyes, all the material
inlay
suffused in sun, sheets of glass. Replace the canvas where what we
say
about what we see streams into the scene like the archangel's word.

To Autumn

Cayenne and tomatoes red clear through as though the sun split
    And threatened to spoil if not cooked right then and there,
Skin scalded, seed scraped, juice drained, core slit,
    Pulp simmered to sauce with basil, raucous beyond any care,
That runs riot in thyme, rue and bee balm outside the kitchen
window;
    Scattered squash blooms, pollen yellow, scale the prickled stalk,
        Bush beans strip to a few leaves scored with mosaic nicotine,
    Long fingered clusters swollen at knuckles that bend and lock;
Morning glories, twisting under our gaze all summer, now outgrow
The hollow corn and open shocking sky struck eyes of rice and indigo,
        While yellowjackets mine windfall apples to gorge their
        harrowed queen.

I couldn't say I never saw her afternoons in back
    Spreading seed broken from round hearts of hollyhocks
Or caught in the corner of an eye while I folded the laundry stack,
    A shadow that fired young sourwood down by the rocks
To spark and scatter scarlet pins against the royal heaven,
    But she trails her fingers through beds gone all to wisp
    and weeds
        And follows a woman's row, turning back the seamed
        and parted part,
Thread pulled from root and caught with a quick stitch:
it's her given
    Work that's never done or put away, by bowls and mops,
    in sleep or deeds;
    She sorts ripe from green, tired as the worn out child she cleans
    and feeds
        And always pressed, opens the door to a breeze, the air
        her art.

Where else would the sharp early notes be gone, buzzing low
around her,
    Tuned like the lucent green tree frogs with suction cup feet, but
    now bereft,
Turned brown as paper sacks, brittle with the heat; their liquid
songs founder,
    Rough and muzzy, vibration in a bottle with a scant measure of
    water left.
The mouth that covers it blows a deeper tone to call the wanderers in,
    Home from the bars and rosy clouds, hoarse and dizzy but free
    from harm
        Unless the rip of her saw or rasp will slip and cast us back to
        rise
Past the central aster's bezel and ravelled petals, to be a skink asleep in
lizard skin:
    She forms feathers from the scales, curves a horn beak, tacks a
    winged arm,
    Swallows us whole in her black eyes, blood flushed vermillion,
    brilliant and warm,
        While we gather, lift, whistle together, a light wind aloft in
        the sinking skies.

Apparent Matter

Under one arm a basket of wet laundry
for the dryer, in the other a paper sack—
children's pajamas, toothbrushes, paperbacks, sundry
pieces pass between them, packed and unpacked.
Her voice rushes in, layered, likely pleased
at the crush of leaves underfoot, the wrack
and rain when they all let go their trees to feed
the ground. The crack of her step on a dry stick
reminds him how any join can snap apart with ease
like her shoulder blades when she pulls off her coat
or clothes pegged to the line in winter. One matter, then another.
So he steps to take the bags she hands over, quick
calls the children, clears the counter, appeases her further —
Come on, bring in the wash. Matter matters. You're their mother.

Villanelle on Two Lines from Frost

Now fall has turned the first leaves light and let the others stay
the darkest green they'll ever get.
They are that that talks of going / But never gets away.

She dreams a gale that rips up rooted oak and smashes clay
to smithereens. They stop and fret
now fall has turned. The first leaves light and let the others stay

in place. A crash. Awake, they see a trunk lose ground, then sway
and capsize overhead. Forget
they are that that talks of going but never gets away.

The children hear their father's reckless voice condemn the day:
who owes whom the rougher debt,
now? Fall has turned the first leaves. Light and let the others stay

Out of harm's way. Shade goes up in chainsaw spit and spray;
a bitter grinding saps regret.
They are that that talks of going / But never gets away.

Steer clear of all the old mistakes, cut to the bone, and say
drink the dregs, swear by sweat,
now fall has turned the first leaves light and let the others stay:
They are that that talks of going / But never gets away.

Cruel Lament for Elms

Giants who ringed the first place I recall,
your steep shade clean leaved on my dormer wall,
your trunks, the stems of solitude, consoled
as though you could unsay the hot and cold
retorts my parents pitched to hit our peeling clapboards.
Your seeds in winged samaras spun to glove their words.

O exhaling elms, in synchrony I breathed
your air for seven years. Your gray bark sheathed
me even as your farthest branches bent
to sickles, leaves furling a blood brown tent.
I made myself your green shoot grown out long and thin,
a whip escaped the pruning hook, your rootless kin.

Beneath my bed or in a frass-rich tree
infected with the fungus *Graphium ulmi*
hosted by the swarming beetle borers,
I hid from fury with my whelmed restorers.
In forty years my mother's scarred and x-rayed skin
would drain bacilli burgeoning her abdomen.

Virgin *ulmus* rose clear fifty feet
when the first branch broke their sky retreat.
Larvae left their scions laid to ground
for blight. Poor mother cried without a sound.
Van Doren was her name, until my father banned
it like contagion brought in from the netherland.

They cut too soon. Before diseases fell your urn-
shaped canopies, I yearn, I beg: return, learn, burn.

The Struggle Back

At Chartres

The Portals

At Chartres the saints and apostles walk not among
But just above us. We might touch a hem, so close,
Soft rippled black with the air of Paris. Ash has clung
And settled on a smooth brow, straight nose,
Lips so curved and full we know
Nothing will erode or decompose
Their cool compassion, the perfect ratio.
Only a glance strikes out of stone
As we pass under flights of angels that flank the arch.
Stranger and stranger, nine ranks toward the throne,
They carry the nebulous bundles we could wish
To bless, our souls bare before skin, hair, nail or bone.
 Walking away we're awkward, made of mud,
  As if we were rock and they robed and winged in blood.

The Mary Chapel

The Black Madonna whiled the winter
Away in the vaults' dark melancholic empathy
Alone with those who lit a candle and spoke a prayer.
Stretched wide as any mother, she fostered each entreaty
That, descending through frozen stone, reached the catacomb.
Pearwood, lifesize, charred by a torch, in the revolution's century
She vanished before they brought her to flame up from the tomb
At the turn of the sun. A rose that by its beauty
May atone the thorn, she flowers at the bitter root
That the pure may amend the false, the happy
The miserable, that a daughter may bear the fruit
Which sets a mother free. You do not replace her with piety.

Way of life, port of health, star of the sea, all injuries healed,
She slumbers still, a garden closed, a fountain sealed.

The Nave

In saris and silk suits the wedding guests arrive from everywhere.
Clusters of two or three, they whisper under the great blue rose.
A father lifts his boy to the font and drenches his black hair
With handfuls of water generous as the Indus here transposed.
This way the lotus goddess Shri Lakshmi, mother of creation,
Treats her best loved sons, Mud, Moisture and Royal Fortune.
The bride and her gray mother, in a cloud of female relations,
Cross to Mary's chapel. The new statue hails those who importune
With a dip of her glitter scepter so slight it could be fabrication,
Reflection from the rack of prayer candles in the jeweled fist.
She balances the golden child like an emblem and invocation
Lotus born, lotus thighed, standing on lotus, lotus eyed, the lotus
kissed.

   When she lowers her hand she will touch the fingertips to show
   The secret nature of all in all, inside the palm we know we know.

Quitting Byzantium

Four

What was to come is passed. Their clockwork sprung,
My broken teeth rattle under metal skin.
I'd wind all back to draw an airy lung,
The soft elastic pull of the outside in.
Old creature, sing without a breath a song
Of form, a form of words, a word again
To begin the way that atoms began, cold
Then warmed in hands to rosy flesh from gold.

Three

I turn a pliant back on eternity,
Its lidless pupils fixed on a scrimmed lamp.
Run reels reverse for the last dim century:
The shuttle settles back to the cradle ramp
And bottles part in lunar gravity.
There's alchemy in ash past fire, the stamp
Of opalescent kiln, raku cracked palms
Cupped, a mosaic apse to catch sad psalms.

Two

Now where? The tesserae scatter out of order;
Their color, line and patterned grid lie broken.
A ruin, golden finish stripped, my treasure
Chipped to raw clay, raises a blurred token
To beauty, cobalt blue in carib water.
We love best the lost and never spoken
Antique hymn, whose glamour we pursue
To the verge of a wood at night that calls adieu.

One

If I follow, where would we emerge
But back on shore, falling to the summer sea
Dead drunk on the hormone-rich salt surge
Of sexes, the chanted mantra of gull and manatee.
Can one swim the word lords' flood? They urge
Us from the ocean edge, tattered, clapping, free
Of temporal bother. Let loose skin, lace bone
Be witness to our sailing on alone.

Winged Victory

Samothrace, Paris

In the vaulted landing where the great steps remand
She leans into the wind, expands, lifts a heel
From the slabs of marble and rough cut granite
At the cliff edge of a harborless, mountainous island,
Where Poseidon views the Trojan catastrophe,
Sacred to the Cabeiri, demon gods of breath, body and wit.

Armless, she arches in the dusty updraft of the stairwell.
The shiver of our wings blinds us as we advance,
Tranced like new hatched moths that flock
And wheel around her. Her left hand raised, she would compel
Wind, water, the Greek fleets; with the right, annihilate circumstance—
Ptolemy's navy, the waves, sailors and galley slaves tumbled in
deadlock.

From the vacant globe of her polished head, rolled to extinction,
She judges the city named the same as brazen youth, a firebrand
Who could have had power or wisdom but settled for Helen.
We stream before her, pilgrims and persons of distinction
Who seek the favor and intimacy of gods. Her tunic is planned
For drapery blown back over a perfectly natural limb.

Active, veined, ideal, warm, we would step into her cast,
Leap to the open window, nirvana where we wake, watch, wait,
Cast aside arms and head with the weight of the transitory
And hold rock steady two hundred decades in the wicked blast—
Could mere vigil convince the gods to rescind our vegetable fate
Vanquished, victim, beaten a split second in the wing of victory.

Lunanelle

Her light wings recalled green silk, thin paper,
a swallowtail that fiddled sight to be a leaf.
Last night the moon's own moth flew to capture

delight. Like Diana herself out after
hours, she neither ate nor slept: the relief
of green thinned past recall, light as paper

alight on day-glow silk. Between wings a softer
white body cast a furred reflection, thief
of the moon's own. Last night, due to capture

polite moth discourse, she feigned laughter.
Without a mouth she beat and tuned her brief
green light. She called silk, wings; wings, paper

—her slight transparent marks. Wind lifted her
over macadam roads toward the bright pupal grief
of the moon. Mother-sown one last night, she'll capture

in flight rapture's quarter bow. Hunters see all suffer.
Streaked from Mare Vaporum to a windshield reef,
her green wings light the wreck, calling out on paper:
Last night the moon's own moth flew to capture.

Phantom Pantoum

Outer Banks Correspondences

By the mist light of morning, trees still drip
back in the woods; moss rises, clarified, the color
of spring wheat. Pigment this vivid has zipped
and locked in every molecule a meta metaphor.

Back in the wood mosses rise clear, fired the color
New World maps give a land mass: a reef, alive.
Locked in spiral molecules, a meadow metaphor
for topology is a star spread pattern. Bryophytes derive

new worlds; a map gives land its mass, relief, a life
beyond what she can see. Take typography as pretense
for topology—star-spread patter fills pages so rife
with serifs she can't read the letters, only eke out sense—

beyond what? She sees him take, type, graph a sentence
in touch: moss for miss, less, pass, loss. Some may land
with seraphim, but she won't read his letters. They keep sense
hanging from the arctic circle. His country is a thin strand

out of touch. Moist by mist, lest, past, lost, some land
divided by channels or lakes. The rain caught in moss,
hung from the arctic. She circles the country, a thin sand
the Baltic washes up on shore. The quaking bog they cross

divides channels, breaks the rain. Wrought in frost,
Class *Musci* morphed to music. He's old where
the Baltic washes. On shore, their monologue has crossed
to tones that follow *Finlandia*'s ice saga and float midair.

At last music formed from mania. It foretold the aria
spring heat sings, a mantra so dizzy she must stop.
Before the floes of Finland's icy topos, notes midair,
by the missed light of morning, even tundra trees will drop.

Dame Julian in a Hazelnut

The Maker

We need to have knowledge of this
and to naught everything that is made.
A little round thing like a ball
spins in the palm of her hand.
She sees it as a marble, a nutshell,
ready to roll from where we stand
and be lost. But what's inside it?
All matter sinks down to sit
there, compressed: breath and wit
sucked out of the electrons' orbit.

The Lover

See, I am in all things . . .
See, I never remove my hands from my works.
The rest is space, the unmade bed of everything.
Empty into it. A naked touch,
a breeze, circles each inch
of skin, our unbroken covering,
at once. No open or closed,
no cloth, hair, muscle, or bone,
only the hazel in solid stone
where we float still as a posed
universe, packed, touching to every cell
the void outside, and inside the well.

The Keeper

Prayer ones the soul to God.
For love which is never slaked,
the marble rolled, but not away.
The nutmeat ached
for the shell, the pearl longed
for the perfect fit.
The new moon will not be wronged
lying in the old moon's unlit
arms. With her nacre eye
she glazes a grain that frets
her flesh. Now she sees why
a showing is sweet with secrets.

Dogwood Alarm

By pairs and threes they crash
and spin to the shoulder, drivers
stunned, unable to keep their eyes,
wheels, the tingle in their fingertips
from bark and open drifts of silk,
the looseblown momentary bloom.

April. They pass, retreat sideways,
floating away from the little accident.

A specimen tree in a suburban yard
is one thing, fertilized, gravid, buds
popped out all over, azaleas snapping
at its knees. But the woods at the edge
of plowed fields are another story, a waltz
at the dogwood diner, the dance that slays us:

Four or five flowers hover over a branch,
crossed, notched, whiter than this world allows.

photo by Chris Potter

Margaret Rabb works as the art director of a small multimedia design studio and teaches as a visiting lecturer in the Creative Writing Program at the University of North Carolina in Chapel Hill. She lives with her family in the rural Piedmont countryside. Her work has received the *Louisiana Literature* Prize for Poetry, the Phyllis Smart Young award from *The Madison Review*, the *Lullwater* Prize for Poetry, the Hackney Literary Award from the Writing Today conference, and the Charles B. Wood Award for Distinguished Writing from the *Carolina Quarterly*. Her chapbook, *Figments of the Firmament*, was selected by Richard Jackson as winner of the 1998 North Carolina Writers' Network Harperprints Chapbook Competition.

New Issues Press Poetry Series

James Armstrong, *Monument in a Summer Hat*
Anthony Butts, *Fifth Season*
Gladys Cardiff, *A Bare Unpainted Table*
Lisa Fishman, *The Deep Heart's Core Is a Suitcase*
Edward Haworth Hoeppner, *Rain Through High Windows*
Josie Kearns, *New Numbers*
Lance Larsen, *Erasable Walls*
David Dodd Lee, *Downsides of Fish Culture*
Deanne Lundin, *The Ginseng Hunter's Notebook*
Joy Manesiotis, *They Sing to Her Bones*
David Marlatt, *A Hog Slaughtering Woman*
Paula McLain, *Less of Her*
Malena Mörling, *Ocean Avenue*
Julie Moulds, *The Woman With a Cubed Head*
Marsha de la O, *Black Hope*
C. Mikal Oness, *Water Becomes Bone*
Margaret Rabb, *Granite Dives*
Rebecca Reynolds, *Daughter of the Hangnail*
John Rybicki, *Traveling at High Speeds*
Diane Seuss-Brakeman, *It Blows You Hollow*
Marc Sheehan, *Greatest Hits*
Angela Sorby, *Distance Learning*
Russell Thorburn, *Approximate Desire*
Martin Walls, *Small Human Detail in Care of National Trust*
Patricia Jabbeh Wesley, *Before the Palm Could Bloom:*
    Poems of Africa